Love Letters From The Apocalypse

AF624623

John Flynn

BookLeaf Publishing

Presentation by *BookLeaf Publishing*

Web: www.bookleafpub.com

E-mail: info@bookleafpub.com

ISBN: 9789357215442

First edition 2022

To my children. Follow your dreams and never lose that twinkle. Dad loves you.

And to Chef Tom, without you, I wouldn't have been here to write this.

PREFACE

By living my dream putting this into print, I hope to inspire my readers to do the same. I hope that you will experience the same myriad of emotions reading this that I had writing this. I wanted to write an eclectic mix of poetry that spanned different genres of horror, all the way to slasher. Please forgive me, I just had to. Thank you and enjoy.

De-Parted

Her eyes, her eyes
The truth lay in those eyes
Of terror, of lies
Of all I despise
Those eyes, those eyes
Those lovely blue eyes
That I keep beside me
In a jar as my prize
Her lips, her lips
Those ruby red lips
That kiss, that pout
That took fleeting sips
Those lips, those lips
Are forever my lips
As I have sewn them on me
Her sips are my sips
Her heart, her heart
Her beautiful heart
I kept as my valentine
As I tore her apart
My love, my love
My ill-fated love
Though you're buried below
With me, you're above
Your voice, your voice

Your tormenting voice
Still screams through my head
Though I made the right choice

Man's Best Friend

Here I sit, decay all around
The dead and ash cover the ground
How I ponder how life could be
If another were here to survive with me
But alas alone, I wander the street
For water, a blanket, and some food to eat
The moans of the suffering echo away
In the empty expanse of this city today
I fight, then I hide, and rest when I can
In this world overrun by this new form of man
Diseased or undead, whatever you label
Twisted, deformed, and mentally unstable
And careful I am, when it's time for a fight
A fight, for my life, that I'll lose with one bite
Never in one place for more than a day
The need to move on always holds sway
For they stagger along looking for flesh
And if I stop moving, my flesh will be next
So onward alone, I persevere for tomorrow
Keeping my focus, pushing down sorrow
Knowing my focus will keep me alive
My animal instincts will help me survive
I see my someone out in the fog
Though dead, he's my master, and I am his dog

Guilt: Dearly Departed

I hear you calling
Calling my name
Yet you are not here
But the voice is the same
I see you breathing
Through my wood paneled floor
See the blood that stains
The inside of my door
Hear the crying inside
The stall of the shower
And a gurgling sound
Until I shut off the power
And a thumping, A thumping?
But from where does this come
A constant beating
Like the one from a drum
You must be alive
For that is your heart
Yet I have found nothing
Through my house torn apart
That beating, the cadence
Oh, when will this end?
It drives me towards madness
As my will starts to bend
Sleep has not come

For at least seven days
I stagger through life
In an unending daze
When finally, they come
And breach through stained door
I lay screaming and naked
On my wood paneled floor
Where is she, where is she?
I screamed at the men
As the cadence of your heart
Beat again and again
The crying came screaming
From the stall of my shower
And the gurgling resumed
As they turned on my power
I laughed maniacally
As I looked to the sky
I remember it was my hand
That caused you to die
As they dragged your remains
From the rear of my house
I giggled, for I realized
I hated that blouse
The divide between us
Caused me to crack
Taking an action
I could never take back
But I was not crazy
Not as crazy as you

The knife through my throat
Was clear as day
It popped out of the bag
As they hauled me away
I turned and saw you
Smiling with glee
So happy in the madness
You inspired in me
I smiled as well
For in death, we're restarted
For you will always be
My dearly departed

The Long Walk

This path I walk feels never-ending
Always winding, always bending
My soul's been stripped of all its hue
Still, I walk on after losing you
I stop to feel a fleeting breeze
I sit to rest my aching knees
For this journey has taken a toll
Upon my body, upon my soul
This path I walk is what is left
Of a promise that must be kept
For I must search, and I must see
If I have surviving family
Separated by time in hell
And the damned that now on this Earth dwell
I walk alone through fire and rain
Pushing onward through the pain
Not knowing what awaits at home
Is it all for nothing that I roam
Or will my children greet me there
And we resume with loving care
Or have they met the same fate as you
And met their end nightmare come true
Suddenly I caught a chill
As the night was no longer still
I was no longer on this path alone

And I was still so far from home
I grew careless daydreaming
Of reuniting my life with meaning
I pulled my bat and fought the horde
Desperately seeking leave from discord
When at last I was finally free
I ran while sobbing quite deeply
For if I lost every one of you
I do not know how I'd continue
At last, I made it, one whole month gone
But as I approached, everything felt wrong
The house was shattered in mass disrepair
My terror permeated the night's cold air
When at last I made it through the front door
Their grandmother was torn apart on the floor
I walked over her remains to the kitchen
I saw many things, including knives, missing
I knew that I was not alone in the house
So silently I moved as if a mouse
I made it as far as the cellar door
When I heard a small voice implore
Mister, that door is locked for our safety
I turned to the voice and saw little Katie
Our eyes met and we both sighed and cried
She told me the story of the night everyone died
We sat and cried some more on the floor
Then she told me who lay just beyond the locked door
Little Timmy was bitten and turned overnight

She couldn't kill him, so she just hid him from sight
Locked away to keep them both safe
Though the stress of it all was betrayed by her face
At first light we set off with vigor renewed
Reunited at last, and hopeful us two
That somewhere out there a home we shall find
Before we are bitten. Or both lose our minds
For this journey feels its only began
Or are we the last ones in this ending of man
Either way, reunited, we will face it together
Until we find peace or fall into forever
Til again we see her mom and my son
And the closure of what's just begun

One Bite

A bite, one bite, will lead you to forever
Your resistance is weak as you fall to the nether
One bite, one taste, so sweet unto me
To follow, no sorrow, as you awaken to see
The changes in you, as I make you whole
You take your first taste and abandon your soul
I explain what we are and what you must do
And show you the full gift I have given to you
We sleep through the day, then take to the night
We stalk our prey, and you learn how to feed right
Suddenly you stop, as if you were frozen
Then turn to ask me why you were chosen
I tell you simply with earnest, I was captivated
And I wanted to save you after my hunger was sated
I wanted to keep your beauty forever
To keep by my side, as my bride of the nether
She took it all in as she walked to my right
Silently thinking as we walked through the night
After a while she looked over and nodded her head
No expression, just acceptance, of the words I had said
She again looked forward, then up to the sky

She took my hand in hers and released a small sigh
I will be yours forever, but I am your one
There will be no others, for I am no object of fun
I accept your choice, but do you accept mine
That I am no object, to be replaced over time
I smiled and said, your beauty is sublime
Why on earth would I replace this goddess of mine
She smiled and said to those words I hold true
I am now yours forever, or until we pass through
We hunted and loved for many long years
Never a day had passed, that I drove her to tears
We had a bliss so becoming, a perfect forever
We had never a moment of anger together
We traveled the seas, saw the sights in all lands
Always taking our time, for we have time on our hands
And every evening I awaken to a beautiful sight
I'm so grateful and it all began with one bite...

The Master's Lament pt. 1: Jenavieve

On this night of Samhain
On All Hallows Eve
I mourn for my loss
Of my sweet Jenavieve
The hunters took haste
As well as her head
For her uncommon taste
For she was undead
If they could see through her fangs
And her eyes black as coal
To her longing for warmth
And her still intact soul
But wait they did not
And hunt they did well
Their mission was simple
To send my Jena to hell
I have lived a long life
Over four hundred years
But this loss is the first
To drive me to tears
So, I make you this promise
As I'm drowning in wine
Oh, my sweet Jenavieve
Your vengeance is mine

The Master's Lament pt 2: The Last Hunter

I found the last hunter
I have fallen the rest
I saved him for last
For he was their best
The hunter was waiting
And he was prepared
But still took me too lightly
So began his nightmare
I took him down quickly
Stopped short of taking his life
I tied up his children
I ravaged his wife
Silent tears trailed down
Showing the pain of my prey
As I drank from his wife
Till her light dimmed away
As I strode to his threshold
I heard but one word "Why?"
Upon my decision
To leave him alive
It's simple good sir
Said my voice calm and clear
You live on as my lesson
To put others in fear

I looked back at his children
And I softened my eyes
I could see their hate
Upon my scarring their lives
Dear children, I started
You know not of your dad
Who killed my dear Jena
And made me real mad
But when you are older
Come knock on my door
Remind me of this day
If I dare to implore
And if you come calling
To collect on my life
As payment for the suffering
Of losing your mother this night
I shall kneel down
Facing down to my floor
And give you my head
So, I can see Jena once more
I then turned away swiftly
Took off into the night
To calmly await
My fate from this plight
Oh Jena, I miss you
Your vengeance I'd sworn
Though now it's completed
Still empty, I mourn

The Master's Lament pt. 3: The Demise

Twenty years have passed my love
Since you were sent to your maker above
Nineteen years since revenge was bourn
And a pair with revenge on me was sworn
Two will pass my threshold this night
I wish them peace, I will not fight
A promise made long ago will be
For their fury, my head, in trade from me
Oh how I miss you, my one true mate
Oh, how these boys suffered from my hate
But now they have come to collect
The head I promised as my debt
I wear my best and sit with pride
Holding a locket with your face inside
In just minutes, I long to see
You standing there in front of me
To reunite with you once more
Upon my entering death's dark door
To have you there to guide the way
I do not fear, do not dismay
The end I'll so have to rear
As these men hasten my end from here
So onward now to face my fate
To face these men so full of hate

For my sins of ruination
My atonement is decapitation
So I fall to my knees and close my eyes
Brother one speaks to my surprise
Dear Sir, a reunion is what you await
On this, there is no debate
Our father took your love from you
And at first we came here to kill you too
But alas, to make this right sir, you should live
For only a gift would your death by my hand give
For death is truly what you desire
But, why would I grant what gives you fire
For our mother was so kind and grand
Yet she was the one whom was killed by your hand
So on this day, we give you life
For the taking of our fathers wife
If you really still miss your love after this long
Take your own life, coward, and just be gone
Or suffer with life, away from your mate
To live with the fate that came from your hate
It became so silent, I heard the clock tick
They left in a flash with just a door click
I lifted my head and was so alone
I processed his words, now no chance to atone
Kept from our reunion grand
For I did not meet death by his hand
But in my heart we will meet once more

So I picked myself up off the floor
Walked up to the roof and awaited dawn
I’m coming dear Jena, it’s time to move on

By Demons Be Driven

Through deathless eyes
And windless skies
A soul unforgiven
By demons be driven
What cannot be
Death's dreams unseen
A life forsaken
A score more taken
Run, come undone
Flee from the one
Shaking and breaking
Grave undertaking
Eye of the storm
Armor past worn
Untold admission
By Demons be driven
Soul faded black
From false attack
Life for retaking
And your unmaking
Still don't listen
Tears to glisten
Darkness born arisen
By demons Imprisoned

Visions

Visions of blood
Visions of hatred
The people, the places
So tainted, once sacred
Visions of violence
Visions of fear
All lifeless bodies
Of those once held dear
Visions so haunting
Visions so dire
Of those I have dispatched
For inspiring my ire
My visions take action
My actions take place
My actions cause sorrow
As we meet face to face
My visions so vivid
My visions are haunting
But to finish this path
The tasks are quite daunting
My visions, my nightmares
Have driven my cause
And once, but a moment
I've given to pause
I think and I ponder

But after the wait
My visions consume me
And I'll seal your fate
And as your light is fading
I have visions ten score
And before you stop breathing
I've moved on once more

Mr. Vernon, The Vermin

The man was strapped upon a wall
His screams in vain echoed down the hall
A man came in and said, Mr. Vernon
You might be the worst of this world's vermin
I'll teach you a lesson, you can finish with pride
You'll be changed forever, if you indeed survive
Mr. Vernon cried out, oh what must I do
To escape this night of hell with you
To teach you a lesson since you diddled a child
You must lose the weapons you chose to run wild
to unlock your fate, wrapped around your wrists
are the blades, of which, you lose your fists
With that its almost over as my trap will release
But you have one last thing before this night will cease
You must cauterize your wounds in battery acid

To ensure, your intentions, like your cock remain flaccid
Vernon yelled and cursed to no avail
it was about the time to finish his tale
The young trap maker now sported an erection
As Mr. Vernon triggered Natural Selection
A demon returned to hell, so many more to send
This was just the beginning, nowhere close to the end

Lone Survivor

Out there hiding in the reeds
The lone survivor from my deeds
Hoping to stay out of sight
But I chose you to live on this night
My first victim lost his head
Both two and three, I stabbed them dead
Four was crushed between jamb and door
Five bled out on the dining room floor
Number six died with his guts hanging out
Seven died choking while flailing about
Eight was great, so I did it again
So, nine like eight, met a quite gruesome end
Well, back to our survivor, oh dear number ten
Hiding amongst the reeds, in her watery den
Praying to God that I'll only walk by
And not meeting an end, like the others who've died
But alas, dear victim, you may live on this day
And move through your live in grand disarray
Oh, tell my legend, so all can hear
So, millions can travel this region in fear
I now will move on and leave you this day
And find some new victims just down the way
For your friends helped me scratch an itch
But I'm really itchy and life is a bitch

Second Survivor

The second story's the same as the first
Of a survivor, who's life I have cursed
Now that, down the way, I've arrived
Nine souls died and one survived
Victim one, mysteriously drowned
Victim two's parts are in the ground
Number three was dumb as hell
Was impaled and broken as she fell
Number four was killed with ease
Ignored her crying please, please, please
Number five stole number six's flower
Plastered their parts all over the shower
Seven died trying to be the hero
Eight combusted, survival rate zero
My last victim, dear number nine
Had his life ended dreadfully unkind
My machete dislodged most of his mind
And as for my witness, dear number two
Horribly scarred like the one before you
In the crawlspace of cabin three
Curled in a ball, waiting for me
But alas, how time is fleeting
It was never you I was seeking
Into the shadows, I now must leave
To find a new chapter of torment to weave

Through survivors, my story grows
Who's in chapter three, no one knows
But I promise you this, as I leave, taking flight
You didn't outsmart me; I chose you this night

My Nightmare Before Christmas

Twas the night before Christmas and all through my house
Zombies were stumbling and bumbling about
The cantrips were hung by the stairway with care
So, if they tried to come up, we would know they were there
In the attic, our children slept snug in their beds
With Louisville sluggers right next to their heads
My wife had her shotgun, for me Smith and Wesson
If those bastards came upstairs, we would teach them a lesson
Then out on the lawn came a mighty loud howl
God damn it, now werewolves were out on the prowl
I lamented this night, our holiday curse
How we could end up undead or much worse
Then came screaming from right down the way
They must have got Jonas and his kids, Jim and May
Then way down the street came a roar and a clatter

I braced myself to see what NOW, was the matter
But what, in front of my eyes did appear
A battalion of soldiers with a tank at their rear
At the top of that tank was general McTodd
Shooting at zombies and commanding his squad
Franklin and Watts cut us our way
Nichols, cover their six with some ruthless gunplay
The rest find anyone who's been lucky so far
Give them food, a blanket, and a seat in a car
As he spoke his eyes caught sight of my house
He saw me in my T-shirt and my wife in her blouse
Soldiers' bee line that house over there
To save a family that's stuck at the top of their stairs
The soldiers fought hard, though they numbered but thirty
But they had some cool tricks, most clean, but some dirty
The zombies were easy, they fell in a line
The wolves were a bitch, but they fell over time
At last, they reached our humble abode
And helped us carry some things and our kids to the road
As we reached the rear guard and set off to the night

We heard the General yell “Another family saved, now let’s fight the good fight”

Seven Doors

The smell came from the other side of the door
The rotting familiar, I had smelled this before
Six doors so far had marked this case
Bodies, dismembered, all over the place
Yet, so savvy, had not left a clue
'Cept for watercolors of crimson he left in the loo
As I entered, I saw her, well at least what was left
In piles, most equal, for this psycho was deft
Her head in the middle, looking up to the sky
On the ground in four piles, the rest of her lie
But her head was placed there with purpose
For there were words left on that surface
On the ceiling, finally, their silence was broken
So haunting, so brazen, I could hear the words spoken
Mr. Detective, you have followed me here
But as with the five others, no clues will appear
As you've studied me, I've studied you all
And you, unlike me, shall suffer this fall
For all this has been fun, but I've had my fill
When your phone rings, it will reveal my last kill
And so, it will end behind seven doors

Five piles of human, on seven strange floors
I will leave you with words left unspoken
And a lesson that will leave you forever broken
It was but a minute and then I heard my phone
ring
I said hello and then braced for the news it
would bring
In a moment my footfalls, in another, tires
tearing
Speeding down the street, lights on, sirens
blaring
I see the blues from two blocks away
I pull up to see the yellow tape out on display
I walk up the porch and through my now open
door
My hopes and dreams were spread out on the
floor
A familiar five piles, a more than familiar head
In those five piles, my wife now lay dead
I choke back a sob and survey the scene
To hopefully find a clue yet unseen
I walked my house with the CSI
Inwardly I said my final goodbye
Finally, on my fridge I saw the envelope
As I read it, I felt a loss of my hope
Dear detective, I am now retired
And your investigation is now expired
In this, my final work, I am sending
That there's no such thing as a happy ending

I have been with you this entire crime
Watching in earnest, biding my time
But alas, the tie, must be severed
My best for your future endeavors
As I finished, my legs were unstable
Shaking, I sat at my kitchen table
Mourning my loss, mourning defeat
Failing as this man's work was complete
A final tear fell at my ruined life
A single tear for my fallen wife
A prayer, a promise, and faith renewed
And no rest until I've ended you

Mirror Image

The person, holds your visage akin
She has you same voice and wears your same skin
But a darkness befallen has rendered a toll
Is it the same person, now lacking a soul
Or has the visage come from a place unclear
To take over the body of once whom I held dear
A doppleganger of darkness befell who once was the light
Then damned from the day, and lived but at night
There's no mistaking the mirror image that stands before me
But surely, it's not the person who you used to be
Dictated by rage, an emulsion of hate
Walking with an anger that dictates your gait
Blue eyes once soft now pointed with lies
The torture that's wafting is what I despise
Holding the living up over my head
Hoping the stress will have me drop dead
I sit scanning your face still holding out hope
Praying for a lifeline, a heavenly rope

That rope was a dream, never to come
Head in hands, I sit silent, solemn
I need an escape, destination unclear
Some days I wish we would all disappear
No more fighting, inciting, a family broken
By words of hatred, of malice, even ones left unspoken
The lies that have come, ghosts of the past
I'm running against it, in this role I was cast
Fast forward one -year, postmortem, your visage remains
Carnage asunder and your soul bearing stains
Once united, in the present, cast away
Like trash, discarded, in an undignified way
Though change hides transgression
But through careful dissection
I have found the direction
At life's intersection
I shall meet you on the path
Oh, doppelganger, to get my life back
And return to all those, whom your shadow divides
To return them to the light, that forever shines
Your skin will fall and show your visage true
A face full of hate, eyes a ravenous hue

A black twisted mass, from the cancer inside
Forever growing from hate, lust, and lies
But alas I'm looking up at two doors
They stand ominous as the first thing at the top of two floors
They will both swing inwards, then we stand face to face
Somehow, I must stand as a man, life erased
And battle a demon, that wears the skin that was you
A battle that innocents, should never go through
But the demon did not care as this battle progressed
Smug and cocky, oh demon, I will pass the test
Swing, parry, thrust, skilled in your ways
A battle of subterfuge, a judgement that sways
I see the opening, driving truth through
You scream as it's light, shines upon you
And vanquish that mirror image of she
Who longer exists, what will be, will be

Awakening

This aching, undertaking
That screams out my name
This undertaking, backbreaking
Lives' never the same
This shaking, always making
As the day breaks the night
This haunting, task daunting
As the path comes to light
The clearing, never nearing
As the path turns and twists
I hear their crying, undying
As I'm shaking my fists
Eyes searing, never fearing
As I forge on ahead
Eyes blinking, brain thinking
Of all you have said
Never speaking, just seeking
Those that I have lost
And I'm ready, hands steady
To pay whatever the cost
To lose my soul, left unwhole
If that's the price for the lost
Not shattered, just battered
Yet, I am not broken
No longer dreaming, just steaming
The sleeper has awoken

Falling Star

Star light star bright
Star that falls upon us this night
Though wish we may
Though wish we might
There's no escape
From your end of flight
We see you break the atmosphere
The end of your journey coming near
Some loot, some kill, most cower in fear
Yet some just nod and release a tear
Could it be from heaven
On this hour that strikes eleven
This rock falling from up on high
This mass that brings billions to die
That which darkens the sky
This object that will change reality
When at last it lands with a thunderous boom
That rocks the world
A sign death comes soon
The Shockwave alone slams a continents door
And cracks appear on the ocean bed floor
Earth and rock fly towards the sky
Then gravity brings them to where they lie
Acid rain falls to the ground
Millions scream and then no sound

Magma pressures through the ocean bed floor
Through broken mantle and molten core
Life as we know it has gone awry
So few left and billions who died
Those of us left are huddled in bunker
For how long? who knows how long we must
hunker
So, star light, star bright
Who hast hit us with all its might
Though we wish for sun
We wish for light
But are now stuck in forever night.

Within the Woods

Within the woods, evil hums
For something wicked this way comes
Will it have the guise of man
To follow through its chaos plan
Or will a soulless temptress rise
To beguile all those with whom despise
All unbeknownst to this wanderer today
As she treks through the path on her way
She stops in her tracks at one hundred paces
For in the darkened wood, she sees one hundred faces
So, menacing they are, but none make a sound
Before they close in, she puts foot to ground
So, she darts through the dark with uncanny speed
The crashes behind her is all the inspiration she needs
An unnatural growl calls from behind to her right
Her gaze catches the monster that stalks her tonight
Just up ahead is the path to the grove
Yet, she is so far from her home at the cove
She starts chanting a hymn as she breaks into the clear

Just a second behind her is the source of her fear
In an instant she turned, her chanting stopped
One second later, at her feet, the beast dropped
From her cloak she pulls two silver pieces
The lump at her feet, on its back, she eases
As chanting grows behind her, she sets the silver on its eyes
Rain, lightning, and thunder erupt from darkened skies
The rain melts the beast into the form of man
The curse broken in the field where it began
The man coughed and looked up at his long-lost love
As she lovingly looked down on him from above
She set him free from his curse at last
His old life seemed so long in the past
Yet there she sat, looking not one day older
Her beauty was one that looked never to smolder
He pressed his lips to hers as love took him over
He was entranced by his love as they kissed deep and slower
Time stopped for a moment, then a button was pressed
The button was the dagger that entered his chest
I love you he gasped, and his eyes grew wide
As her fangs grew. I love you too she cried
He closed his eyes as she tore into his flesh
She closed her eyes as the dagger finished the rest

As he fell, she smiled, and said you are now free
Then split the body in two for all around to see
The chanting began again, witches numbered two dozen
She disappeared into the fog and rejoined her coven
The fog moved swiftly, and then they were gone
The appearance of evil was now all but moved on
A scream rang out along with the cadence of hooves
And the proof of evil is now outside of the woods

The Hunted

The darkness has followed me once more
Demons screaming, now pleading, outside
my door
A correction of course, that ends in a crash
My own claws extending, ready to slash
To rip, lash out, and tear into two
My own demons screaming, to slash into
you
The first two enter and were torn apart
The next two fell as I tore out their hearts
The rest stopped and stared from outside the
door
I then let out a scream that shook forest
floor
The hunters, now hunted, flee from the
scene
Back into the woods, back into the trees
I do not need sight, as I smell all your fear
It only grows as upon you I near
I ran through them all one by one
Stopping but briefly to admire my fun
Heads literally rolling, intestines trailing
Limbs ripped apart, vital organs failing
When at last, all are fallen
I have peace once more

Gore drops from the trees
Corpses litter forest floor
I make my way back to my cabin
Lay my body in bed
I await the next wave
Of the soon to be dead.

Breathe again

I can finally breathe again
I can finally see the bend
Not lost in the way back when
Now that I can breathe again
A dialogue for answers
Having wasted time
Surviving all the cancers
Planted in my mind
Inhaling newfound freedom
Cherishing the air
Life no longer a museum
Of pain, anger, and disrepair
Step by step it takes me
A journey on new roads
Sifting through leaves of tea
To see how life decodes
Broke free from Poseidon
Emotions to unpack
Sunrise breaks the horizon
Darkness left in back
One more stop can save me
If I arrive on time
No one left to stop me
I paused to catch your eyes
I'm oh so curious

My past lay furious
You stopped and took my hand
And now I understand
I can finally breathe again
Chains in my heart start to break and bend
I can see where the pain will end
Now that I can finally breathe again

www.ingramcontent.com/pod-product-compliance
Lightning Source LLC
Chambersburg PA
CBHW051739130826
49812CB00033B/928
9789357215442